Liberate Your Life Persor Strategies for a Joyf

Fanny Crosby

Copyright © [2023]

Title: Liberate Your Life Personal Development Strategies for a Joyful Existence
Author's: Fanny Crosby

This book was printed and published by [Publisher's: **Fanny Crosby**] in [2023]

ISBN:

Table of content

Chapter 9: Enhancing Personal Growth Through Learning

The Lifelong Learning Mindset

Expanding Your Knowledge and Skills

Seeking Personal Growth Opportunities

Embracing Challenges and Continuous Improvement

Chapter 10: Creating a Joyful Existence

Embracing Positivity and Gratitude

Living in Alignment with Your Values

Celebrating Your Achievements

Spreading Joy and Kindness to Others

Chapter 11: Sustaining Personal Growth in the Long Run

Overcoming Plateaus and Stagnation

Developing a Supportive Network

Embracing Change and Adaptability

Continuing the Journey of Personal Development

Chapter 12: Conclusion 97

Recap of Key Strategies for Personal Development

Final Thoughts on Liberating Your Life

Embracing a Joyful Existence Moving Forward

Chapter 1: Introduction to Personal Development

Understanding Personal Development

In our pursuit of a happy life, personal development plays a crucial role. It is a lifelong journey of self-discovery, growth, and improvement that empowers us to live a more fulfilling and joyful existence. Personal development is not a one-size-fits-all concept; it is a deeply personal and individual process that varies for each person. In this chapter, we will dive into the foundations of personal development and how it can transform your life.

At its core, personal development involves gaining self-awareness and understanding oneself on a deeper level. It requires introspection and reflection to identify our strengths, weaknesses, values, and beliefs. By becoming aware of our thoughts, emotions, and behaviors, we can make conscious choices that align with our true selves and lead to a happier life.

Personal development also encompasses setting and achieving meaningful goals. It involves creating a clear vision of what we want in life and taking intentional steps to make it a reality. By setting specific, measurable, attainable, relevant, and time-bound (SMART) goals, we can stay focused and motivated on our journey towards personal growth.

Furthermore, personal development involves acquiring new knowledge, skills, and habits that contribute to our overall well-being. It encourages continuous learning and self-improvement in various areas of our lives, such as relationships, career, health, and spirituality. By expanding our capabilities and broadening our perspectives, we can unlock new opportunities and experience greater fulfillment.

It is essential to note that personal development is not a linear process. It is filled with ups and downs, setbacks, and challenges. However, these obstacles serve as opportunities for growth and resilience. By embracing failure as a learning experience and maintaining a positive mindset, we can overcome obstacles and keep moving forward on our personal development journey.

Ultimately, personal development is about embracing change and becoming the best version of ourselves. It is about taking responsibility for our lives, making conscious choices, and continuously evolving to create a joyful and purposeful existence.

In the following chapters of "Liberate Your Life: Personal Development Strategies for a Joyful Existence," we will explore various tools and techniques to enhance personal development. From mindfulness practices to effective goal-setting strategies, this book will provide you with practical guidance and inspiration to embark on your personal development journey. Remember, personal development is a lifelong commitment, and with dedication and perseverance, you can transform your life and experience the happiness you deserve.

Why Personal Development Matters

In our fast-paced and ever-changing world, personal development has become more important than ever. It is the key to unlocking a joyful existence and living a happy life. Personal development allows us to grow, evolve, and become the best version of ourselves. It empowers us to take control of our lives and make positive changes that lead to happiness and fulfillment.

So, why does personal development matter? The answer lies in the transformative power it holds. When we engage in personal development, we embark on a journey of self-discovery and self-improvement. We gain a deeper understanding of who we are, what our values are, and what truly makes us happy. This self-awareness is the foundation for personal growth and happiness.

Personal development also helps us develop essential life skills. It enables us to enhance our communication skills, build healthy relationships, and manage our emotions effectively. These skills not only benefit our personal lives but also have a significant impact on our professional success. When we invest in personal development, we become more confident, resilient, and adaptable, allowing us to navigate life's challenges with grace and ease.

Moreover, personal development helps us break free from limiting beliefs and negative thought patterns. We learn to let go of self-doubt, fear, and insecurity, replacing them with self-belief, courage, and positivity. This shift in mindset opens up new possibilities and opportunities, enabling us to create the life we truly desire.

Personal development is not a one-size-fits-all approach. It is a highly individualized journey that varies from person to person. Each one of us has unique strengths, weaknesses, and aspirations. Personal development strategies allow us to tailor our growth to our specific needs and goals. Whether it's practicing mindfulness, setting goals, or learning new skills, personal development provides us with tools and techniques to design our own path to happiness.

In conclusion, personal development matters because it empowers us to live a happy life. It equips us with the skills, mindset, and self-awareness needed to overcome challenges, build meaningful relationships, and achieve personal and professional success. By investing in our personal growth, we can liberate ourselves from limitations and create a joyful existence filled with purpose, fulfillment, and happiness. So, embark on your personal development journey today and liberate your life. The possibilities are endless!

The Benefits of Personal Development

In the pursuit of a happy life, personal development plays a crucial role. It is a continuous journey of self-improvement that allows individuals to unlock their true potential and live a joyful existence. Liberating your life through personal development strategies can bring about transformative changes in various aspects of your life, including relationships, career, and overall well-being.

One of the key benefits of personal development is increased self-awareness. It helps you gain a deeper understanding of your strengths, weaknesses, and values. This self-awareness enables you to make conscious choices aligned with your authentic self, leading to a more fulfilled and contented life. By identifying your passions and interests, you can pursue activities that bring you joy and fulfillment, further enhancing your overall happiness.

Personal development also enhances your emotional intelligence, enabling you to navigate relationships more effectively. Through self-reflection and self-improvement, you can develop empathy, understanding, and better communication skills. This allows you to build stronger and more meaningful connections with others, fostering a happier and more harmonious social life.

Additionally, personal development strategies empower you to set and achieve meaningful goals. By cultivating discipline, focus, and perseverance, you can overcome obstacles and create a clear path towards your desired outcomes. This sense of purpose and achievement not only boosts your self-confidence but also brings immense satisfaction and happiness.

Moreover, personal development promotes lifelong learning and growth. It encourages you to embrace new challenges, step out of your comfort zone, and acquire new skills and knowledge. This continuous growth not only expands your horizons but also opens up opportunities for personal and professional advancement, leading to a more fulfilling and prosperous life.

Furthermore, personal development strategies enhance your overall well-being. By prioritizing self-care and practicing mindfulness, you can reduce stress, increase resilience, and improve your overall mental and physical health. This holistic approach to personal development ensures that you are not only happy but also leading a healthy and balanced life.

In conclusion, personal development is an essential tool in the pursuit of a happy life. By embarking on this transformative journey, you can unlock your true potential, cultivate self-awareness, improve relationships, achieve meaningful goals, promote lifelong learning, and enhance overall well-being. Liberating your life through personal development strategies will undoubtedly pave the way for a joyful existence filled with purpose, fulfillment, and happiness.

Setting Goals for Personal Development

In our quest for a happy life, personal development plays a crucial role. It empowers us to grow, evolve, and create a joyful existence. One of the fundamental aspects of personal development is setting goals that align with our desires and aspirations. By setting clear objectives, we can pave the way for a fulfilling journey of self-improvement.

When it comes to setting goals for personal development, it is essential to begin by reflecting on our current state. Take a moment to evaluate various aspects of your life, such as relationships, career, health, and spirituality. Identify areas that require attention and improvement. This self-reflection will help you gain a deeper understanding of where you are and where you want to be.

Once you have identified the areas you wish to develop, it's time to set specific goals. Remember that goals should be realistic, measurable, and time-bound. Set achievable targets that motivate and inspire you, but also allow room for growth. Break down larger goals into smaller, manageable steps to ensure steady progress along your personal development journey.

Furthermore, it is vital to align your goals with your values and passions. Consider what truly matters to you and what brings you joy. By aligning your goals with your core values, you will find greater fulfillment and purpose in your pursuit of personal development.

To ensure success in achieving your goals, it is essential to create a roadmap. Break down each goal into actionable tasks and create a timeline for completion. This will provide structure and direction to your personal development journey. Regularly review and evaluate your progress, making adjustments as necessary. Celebrate your achievements along the way, as acknowledging your growth and accomplishments will fuel your motivation to continue.

Lastly, surround yourself with a supportive and like-minded community. Seek out individuals who are also on a path of personal development and share your goals and aspirations. This network will provide encouragement, accountability, and valuable insights that can accelerate your growth.

Setting goals for personal development is a powerful step towards creating a happy life. It allows us to take control of our destiny and actively work towards becoming the best version of ourselves. Embrace the process, stay committed, and watch as your personal development journey unfolds, leading you to a more joyful existence.

Chapter 2: Self-Awareness: The Foundation of Personal Growth

The Importance of Self-Awareness

Welcome to "Liberate Your Life: Personal Development Strategies for a Joyful Existence." In this subchapter, we delve into the importance of self-awareness and how it can contribute to a happy life. Whether you are a young adult navigating the challenges of early adulthood or a seasoned individual seeking fulfillment, understanding yourself is the key to unlocking a joyful existence.

Self-awareness is the ability to recognize and understand your own thoughts, emotions, and behaviors. It involves being in tune with your strengths, weaknesses, values, and beliefs. While it may sound simple, self-awareness is a lifelong journey that requires continuous self-reflection and introspection.

One of the significant benefits of self-awareness is the ability to make informed decisions that align with your authentic self. When you truly know who you are, you can make choices that resonate with your values and bring you closer to your goals and aspirations. This sense of alignment creates a deep sense of satisfaction and contentment, leading to a more fulfilling and happy life.

Self-awareness also allows you to identify and address any negative patterns or limiting beliefs that may be holding you back. By understanding your triggers and reactions, you can break free from self-sabotaging behaviors and replace them with healthier alternatives. This process of self-discovery empowers you to take control of your life and create positive change.

Moreover, self-awareness enhances your relationships with others. When you understand your own emotions and motivations, you can better empathize with those around you. This empathy fosters deeper connections and promotes harmonious interactions, leading to more fulfilling and meaningful relationships. Nurturing healthy connections with loved ones and cultivating a supportive network is crucial for a happy life.

In conclusion, self-awareness is an essential component for creating a happy life. By understanding yourself on a deeper level, you can make choices that align with your values and aspirations, break free from negative patterns, and foster meaningful relationships. Embrace the journey of self-discovery, and you will unlock the key to a joyful existence. Stay tuned for further strategies and insights in "Liberate Your Life: Personal Development Strategies for a Joyful Existence."

Assessing Your Strengths and Weaknesses

In our journey towards a happy life, it is essential to take a step back and reflect on our own strengths and weaknesses. Self-awareness is the key to personal development and a joyful existence. By understanding our strengths, we can harness them to their full potential, while recognizing our weaknesses allows us to work on improving ourselves.

Strengths are the unique qualities that make us who we are. They are the traits, skills, and abilities that come naturally to us and bring us joy when we use them. Assessing our strengths involves introspection and identifying what we excel at. It could be our communication skills, creativity, problem-solving abilities, or compassion towards others. Recognizing our strengths not only boosts our self-confidence but also provides a roadmap for personal and professional growth. It enables us to focus on areas where we can make a significant impact and find fulfillment in what we do.

On the other hand, acknowledging our weaknesses is equally important. Weaknesses are areas where we may lack proficiency or struggle to perform at our best. Assessing our weaknesses helps us identify areas for improvement and growth. It allows us to be honest with ourselves and embrace opportunities for personal development. By addressing our weaknesses, we can overcome limitations and broaden our horizons, leading to a more fulfilling and happy life.

Assessing strengths and weaknesses is not about dwelling on shortcomings or comparing ourselves to others. It is about self-reflection, acceptance, and growth. Embracing both our strengths and weaknesses helps us become more well-rounded individuals, capable of handling life's challenges with grace and resilience.

To assess your strengths, take some time for self-reflection and ask yourself what activities bring you joy and fulfillment. Consider your past achievements and the skills that helped you succeed. Seek feedback from trusted friends or mentors who can provide insights into your strengths that you may not have recognized. Once you have identified your strengths, find ways to incorporate them into your daily life and pursue opportunities that allow you to utilize them.

To assess your weaknesses, be open to constructive criticism and feedback. Reflect on areas where you feel less confident or encounter difficulties. Seek resources and guidance to help you improve in those areas. Remember, weaknesses are not permanent limitations but opportunities for growth and development.

By constantly assessing our strengths and weaknesses, we can embark on a journey of personal growth and live a more joyful existence. Embrace your strengths, work on your weaknesses, and watch yourself flourish in all aspects of life. Remember, self-awareness is the key to unlocking your true potential and living a happy life.

Identifying Your Values and Beliefs

In the journey towards a happy and fulfilling life, it is essential to explore and understand our values and beliefs. These fundamental aspects shape our thoughts, emotions, and actions, influencing the choices we make and the paths we take. By gaining clarity on our values and beliefs, we can align ourselves with what truly matters to us, leading to a more purposeful and joyful existence.

Values are the guiding principles that reflect what is important to us. They define our priorities and provide a moral compass for decision-making. Identifying our values allows us to live authentically and in harmony with our true selves. They can include honesty, compassion, integrity, loyalty, creativity, or any other qualities that resonate deeply with us. By recognizing our values, we can make choices that are in alignment with who we are, fostering a sense of fulfillment and contentment.

Beliefs, on the other hand, are the deeply ingrained thoughts and convictions we hold about ourselves, others, and the world around us. They shape our perceptions, attitudes, and behaviors, often operating on a subconscious level. Some beliefs can empower us, while others may hold us back. Identifying our beliefs enables us to challenge and transform the limiting ones, replacing them with empowering ones that support our happiness and growth.

To identify your values, take a moment to reflect on what truly matters to you. What principles do you consistently uphold in your life? What qualities do you admire in others? What activities or experiences make you feel fulfilled? Consider writing a list of your values and prioritize them based on their importance to you. This exercise will help you gain clarity and make conscious choices aligned with your values.

Examining your beliefs requires self-awareness and introspection. Pay attention to the thoughts and narratives that run through your mind. Are they empowering or limiting? Are they based on evidence or assumptions? Challenge the beliefs that no longer serve you and replace them with ones that support your happiness and growth. Surround yourself with positive influences, read inspiring books, and seek guidance from mentors or coaches who can help you in this transformative process.

By identifying your values and beliefs, you gain a deeper understanding of yourself and what brings you joy. This self-awareness allows you to make choices that align with your true essence and lead to a more fulfilling and happy life. Embrace this journey of self-discovery, and liberate yourself from anything that hinders your personal growth and well-being.

Cultivating Self-Compassion and Self-Acceptance

In our journey towards a happy life, it is crucial to recognize and embrace our own worthiness. Self-compassion and self-acceptance are powerful practices that can transform our lives and lead us to a more joyful existence. This subchapter will delve into the importance of cultivating these qualities and provide practical strategies for developing self-compassion and self-acceptance.

Self-compassion is the practice of treating ourselves with kindness, understanding, and empathy. It involves acknowledging our own suffering and extending the same compassion we would offer to a dear friend. Often, we are our harshest critics, constantly berating ourselves for our perceived flaws and mistakes. By cultivating self-compassion, we break free from this cycle and learn to embrace ourselves with love and understanding.

One way to cultivate self-compassion is through mindful self-reflection. Take a moment each day to check in with yourself, acknowledging any negative thoughts or emotions without judgment. Instead of criticizing yourself, offer words of comfort and understanding. Treat yourself as you would treat a close friend going through a difficult time, with patience and kindness.

Self-acceptance is closely tied to self-compassion. It is the act of embracing ourselves fully, flaws and all. Often, we strive for perfection and hold ourselves to impossibly high standards. However, true happiness lies in accepting ourselves as we are, with all our imperfections and quirks. Self-acceptance does not mean complacency; it means recognizing our inherent worthiness regardless of external achievements or societal expectations.

To foster self-acceptance, it is important to challenge our negative self-talk and replace it with positive affirmations. Remind yourself daily of your strengths and accomplishments, no matter how small. Surround yourself with positive influences that uplift and support you. Engage in activities that bring you joy and make you feel proud of who you are.

Cultivating self-compassion and self-acceptance requires practice and patience. It is a lifelong journey of self-discovery and growth. As you embark on this path, remember to be gentle with yourself and celebrate every step forward. By embracing self-compassion and self-acceptance, you will liberate yourself from self-doubt and negativity, creating space for a truly joyful existence.

In conclusion, the practice of cultivating self-compassion and self-acceptance is essential for everyone seeking a happy life. It allows us to break free from self-criticism and perfectionism, fostering a deep sense of worthiness and contentment. By treating ourselves with kindness and embracing our true selves, we embark on a journey towards a more joyful existence. Start today by implementing the strategies discussed in this subchapter, and watch as your life transforms into one filled with love, acceptance, and happiness.

Chapter 3: Creating a Positive Mindset

The Power of Positive Thinking

In today's fast-paced and often stressful world, it's easy to get caught up in negativity and lose sight of the incredible power of positive thinking. But what if I told you that adopting a positive mindset can transform your life and lead to a truly joyful existence? Welcome to the subchapter "The Power of Positive Thinking" from the book "Liberate Your Life: Personal Development Strategies for a Joyful Existence."

Positive thinking is not just a cliché; it is a proven strategy for achieving happiness and success. When you focus on the positive aspects of your life, you attract more positivity and abundance. Your thoughts and beliefs shape your reality, so why not choose thoughts that uplift and empower you?

The power of positive thinking lies in its ability to transform your mindset and outlook on life. By cultivating a positive attitude, you open yourself up to new opportunities and possibilities. You become more resilient in the face of challenges and setbacks, as you believe in your ability to overcome them. Positive thinking empowers you to take control of your life and create the happy life you deserve.

Research has shown that positive thinking has numerous benefits for your physical and mental well-being. It reduces stress, boosts your immune system, and improves your overall health. When you think positively, you release feel-good hormones, such as endorphins, that enhance your mood and increase your happiness levels.

But how can you cultivate a positive mindset in a world filled with negativity? It begins with self-awareness and mindfulness. Pay attention to your thoughts and replace any negative or self-limiting beliefs with positive affirmations. Surround yourself with positive people who uplift and inspire you. Practice gratitude daily, focusing on the blessings in your life. Engage in activities that bring you joy and align with your passions.

Remember, positive thinking is not about denying the challenges or difficulties in life. It's about choosing to respond to them with optimism and resilience. By shifting your perspective and focusing on solutions rather than problems, you can navigate through life's obstacles with grace and ease.

In conclusion, the power of positive thinking is a transformative force that can lead to a happy and fulfilling life. Embrace the power within you to cultivate a positive mindset, and watch as your life unfolds with joy and abundance.

Overcoming Negative Self-Talk

In our journey towards a happy life, one of the biggest obstacles we often face is our own negative self-talk. We all have that voice in our head that constantly tells us we're not good enough, smart enough, or deserving of happiness. This self-sabotaging dialogue can be incredibly damaging and can prevent us from reaching our full potential.

But fear not, for in this subchapter, we will explore effective strategies to overcome negative self-talk and reclaim our lives. By understanding the power of our thoughts and learning how to reframe them, we can create a more joyful existence.

The first step in overcoming negative self-talk is to become aware of it. Pay attention to the thoughts that arise in your mind and observe how they make you feel. Are they uplifting or do they bring you down? By recognizing these patterns, you can start challenging and reframing them.

Next, challenge the validity of your negative thoughts. Are they based on facts or merely assumptions? Often, our self-doubt is rooted in irrational beliefs or past experiences that no longer hold true. By questioning the logic behind these thoughts, we can begin to dismiss their power over us.

Once you've identified negative self-talk, it's time to replace it with positive affirmations. Create a list of affirmations that counteract your self-defeating thoughts. For example, if you catch yourself thinking, "I'm not smart enough to succeed," replace it with, "I am intelligent and capable of achieving great things." Repeat these affirmations daily to rewire your brain and cultivate a positive mindset.

Additionally, surround yourself with a supportive network of people who uplift and encourage you. Seek out friends, mentors, or support groups that foster positivity and inspire personal growth. Their influence can help counteract the negative self-talk and boost your self-confidence.

Lastly, practice self-compassion. Treat yourself with kindness and understanding, just as you would a close friend. Remember that nobody is perfect, and it's okay to make mistakes. Embrace your imperfections and celebrate your accomplishments, no matter how small.

By implementing these strategies and making a conscious effort to overcome negative self-talk, you can liberate yourself from the shackles of self-doubt and create a more joyful existence. Embrace the power of positive thinking and watch as your happiness and personal development soars to new heights.

Practicing Gratitude for a Happier Life

In today's fast-paced and ever-changing world, it can be easy to get caught up in the hustle and bustle of daily life. We often find ourselves focusing on what we don't have or what is going wrong, rather than appreciating the abundance and beauty that surrounds us. However, cultivating a mindset of gratitude can have a transformative effect on our lives, leading to greater happiness and fulfillment.

Gratitude is the practice of acknowledging and appreciating the positive aspects of our lives, both big and small. It is a powerful tool that can shift our perspective from one of lack to one of abundance. By consciously focusing on what we are grateful for, we invite more positivity and joy into our lives.

One of the key benefits of practicing gratitude is that it helps us to cultivate a happy life. When we take the time to express gratitude for the things we have, we shift our attention away from what is lacking and towards what is present. This shift in focus allows us to experience greater contentment and satisfaction, leading to an overall sense of happiness.

Gratitude also has a profound impact on our mental and emotional well-being. Research has shown that regularly practicing gratitude can reduce stress, anxiety, and depression. It helps us to cultivate a more positive mindset, enabling us to navigate life's challenges with greater resilience and optimism. By practicing gratitude, we train our minds to look for the silver linings in every situation, fostering a sense of hope and gratitude.

Furthermore, gratitude has the power to enhance our relationships and deepen our connections with others. When we express gratitude towards others, we not only uplift them but also strengthen the bond between us. Gratitude fosters empathy, kindness, and compassion, creating a positive ripple effect that spreads to those around us.

In conclusion, cultivating a practice of gratitude is a powerful strategy for creating a happier life. By appreciating the blessings and abundance in our lives, we shift our focus towards positivity and invite more joy and fulfillment. Gratitude has the potential to transform our mindset, enhance our well-being, and strengthen our relationships. So, let us embark on this journey of gratitude and liberate our lives to experience the true joy and happiness that awaits us.

Cultivating Optimism and Resilience

In the pursuit of a happy life, one must learn to cultivate optimism and resilience. These two qualities are essential in navigating life's ups and downs, and they have the power to transform our existence into a joyful and fulfilling one. In this subchapter, we will explore practical strategies and techniques that can help you develop and strengthen these qualities within yourself.

Optimism is a mindset that enables us to see the silver lining in every situation. It allows us to believe in the possibility of a positive outcome, even in the face of adversity. To cultivate optimism, it is important to practice gratitude regularly. Take a few moments each day to reflect on the things you are grateful for. This simple exercise helps shift your focus towards the positive aspects of life, fostering an optimistic outlook.

Another powerful tool for developing optimism is positive self-talk. Pay attention to the words you use when speaking to yourself and challenge any negative or self-limiting beliefs. Replace them with positive affirmations that reinforce your belief in your abilities and potential. Surrounding yourself with positive and uplifting individuals can also have a significant impact on your optimism levels. Seek out supportive and encouraging relationships that inspire and motivate you.

Resilience, on the other hand, refers to our ability to bounce back from setbacks and face challenges with strength and determination. To cultivate resilience, it is important to develop a growth mindset. Embrace failures and setbacks as opportunities for growth and learning, rather than letting them define you. Set realistic goals and break them down into manageable steps, celebrating each small victory along the way. This will help you build resilience and maintain a positive outlook, even during challenging times.

Practicing self-care is also crucial for cultivating resilience. Engage in activities that bring you joy and help you recharge. This could include hobbies, exercise, spending time in nature, or practicing mindfulness and meditation. Taking care of your physical and mental well-being will provide you with the strength and resilience to overcome any obstacles that come your way.

In conclusion, cultivating optimism and resilience are essential for leading a happy and fulfilling life. By practicing gratitude, positive self-talk, and surrounding yourself with positive influences, you can develop an optimistic mindset. Additionally, embracing failures as opportunities for growth and taking care of yourself through self-care practices will help you build resilience. Remember, with a positive mindset and the ability to bounce back, you can truly liberate your life and create a joyful existence.

Chapter 4: Building Healthy Habits

The Science of Habit Formation

In our journey towards leading a happy life, one of the key factors that can make a significant difference is understanding the science of habit formation. Habits shape our daily routines, behaviors, and ultimately, our overall well-being. Whether we realize it or not, our habits have a profound impact on our happiness levels. By delving into the science behind habit formation, we can gain valuable insights into how to create positive habits that contribute to a joyful existence.

Neuroscientists have discovered that habits are essentially patterns of behavior that become ingrained in our brains. These patterns are formed through a loop consisting of a cue, a routine, and a reward. Understanding this loop can help us understand how habits are created and, more importantly, how to break or change them.

The first step in habit formation is identifying the cue, which is the trigger that initiates the behavior. It could be a specific time of day, a particular situation, or even an emotional state. Once we recognize the cue, we can move on to the routine, which is the behavior itself. This is the part that we can consciously modify. By replacing a negative routine with a positive one, we can create healthier habits that contribute to our happiness.

To reinforce a new habit, it's crucial to identify a reward that provides a sense of satisfaction or pleasure. This reward strengthens the neural pathways associated with the habit, making it more likely to be repeated in the future. By understanding the reward aspect, we can choose rewards that align with our goals and values, ensuring the formation of habits that contribute to our overall happiness.

Breaking old habits can be challenging, but armed with the knowledge of habit formation, we can employ various strategies to make lasting changes. One effective technique is habit stacking, where we attach a new habit to an already established one. This helps create a sense of consistency and makes it easier to incorporate the new behavior into our daily routines.

By understanding the science of habit formation, we empower ourselves to create positive habits that support a joyful existence. Through awareness of the habit loop, identifying cues, consciously modifying routines, and choosing appropriate rewards, we can shape our lives in a way that promotes happiness. Breaking old habits and forming new ones takes time and effort, but with persistence and a solid understanding of the underlying science, we can liberate ourselves from negative patterns and embrace a life filled with joy and fulfillment.

Establishing a Morning Routine

In our fast-paced world, it is easy to overlook the importance of a morning routine. However, having a structured morning routine can significantly contribute to a happy life. It sets the tone for the day, enhances productivity, and helps us approach life with a positive mindset. In this subchapter, we will explore the benefits of establishing a morning routine and provide practical tips to help you create one that works for you.

One of the key advantages of a morning routine is that it allows us to start the day on our own terms. By waking up a little earlier, we can carve out time for self-care and reflection. This time can be used for activities such as meditation, journaling, exercising, or simply enjoying a cup of coffee in peace. By dedicating this time to ourselves, we set an intention for the day and prioritize our well-being. It helps us to focus on what truly matters and avoid getting caught up in the chaos of daily life.

Additionally, a morning routine can increase productivity throughout the day. By starting with a clear mind and a sense of accomplishment, we are better equipped to tackle tasks and make progress on our goals. The morning hours are often the most peaceful and uninterrupted, making it an ideal time for focused work or creative pursuits. With a consistent routine in place, we can make the most of this precious time and set ourselves up for success.

Creating a morning routine that works for you is a deeply personal process. It should be tailored to your unique needs, preferences, and goals. Experiment with different activities and find what brings you joy and fulfillment. Some people find solace in exercise, while others prefer to spend time in nature or read a book. The key is to choose activities that align with your values and leave you feeling energized and inspired.

To establish a successful morning routine, it is essential to prioritize consistency. Set a wake-up time that allows for ample self-care and gives you enough time to complete your desired activities. Avoid hitting the snooze button and resist the temptation of checking your phone first thing in the morning. Instead, use this time to focus on yourself and set positive intentions for the day ahead.

In conclusion, establishing a morning routine is a powerful tool for cultivating a happy life. It offers a precious opportunity to prioritize self-care, promote productivity, and start the day with a positive mindset. By dedicating time to activities that bring joy and fulfillment, you can create a solid foundation for a joyful existence. So, take the first step towards a happier life by designing a morning routine that resonates with you and watch as it transforms your days for the better.

Nurturing a Balanced Lifestyle

In today's fast-paced world, it is easy to get caught up in the hustle and bustle of everyday life, often neglecting our own well-being in the process. However, it is essential to remember that true happiness lies in leading a balanced and fulfilling life. This subchapter aims to provide practical strategies and insights on how to nurture a balanced lifestyle, allowing you to lead a joyful existence.

To achieve a balanced lifestyle, it is crucial to prioritize self-care. Taking care of your physical, mental, and emotional well-being should be at the top of your list. Engaging in regular exercise, eating a nutritious diet, and getting enough sleep are essential for maintaining a healthy body. Additionally, practicing mindfulness and stress-reducing techniques such as meditation or yoga can help calm the mind and promote emotional well-being.

Finding time for hobbies and activities that bring you joy is another crucial aspect of nurturing a balanced lifestyle. In our busy lives, we often forget to make time for things we love. Whether it's painting, gardening, or simply going for a walk in nature, indulging in activities that bring you happiness and fulfillment is essential for maintaining a happy life.

Building and nurturing meaningful relationships is also a key component of a balanced lifestyle. Surrounding yourself with positive and supportive individuals can greatly impact your overall happiness. Take the time to connect with loved ones, engage in meaningful conversations, and create lasting memories together. Remember, a happy life is often built on strong and fulfilling relationships.

Finding a healthy work-life balance is another critical aspect of nurturing a balanced lifestyle. While it is important to dedicate yourself to your career, it is equally important to set boundaries and make time for your personal life. Prioritize your well-being by setting aside time for relaxation, leisure activities, and spending quality time with loved ones.

Lastly, practicing gratitude and cultivating a positive mindset can greatly contribute to a balanced lifestyle. Take the time each day to reflect on the things you are grateful for and focus on the positive aspects of your life. This simple practice can shift your perspective and help you appreciate the beauty and abundance around you.

In conclusion, nurturing a balanced lifestyle is vital for achieving a happy life. By prioritizing self-care, engaging in activities that bring you joy, building meaningful relationships, finding a healthy work-life balance, and practicing gratitude, you can create a life filled with joy, fulfillment, and happiness. Remember, your well-being is the foundation for a joyful existence, so take the time to nurture your mind, body, and soul.

Developing Productivity Habits

In today's fast-paced world, finding ways to boost productivity is crucial for leading a happy life. Whether you're a student, a professional, or a stay-at-home parent, mastering productivity habits can help you achieve your goals, reduce stress, and create a more joyful existence. In this subchapter, we will explore some effective strategies to develop productivity habits that will transform your life.

1. Set Clear Goals: Start by defining your short-term and long-term goals. Having a clear vision of what you want to achieve will give you a sense of direction and purpose, motivating you to stay focused and productive.

2. Prioritize Tasks: Learn to prioritize your tasks based on their importance and urgency. Make a to-do list each day, and tackle the most critical tasks first. By focusing on what needs to be done, you'll avoid wasting time on less important activities.

3. Time Management Techniques: Discover time management techniques that work best for you. Tools like the Pomodoro Technique, where you work for a set period and then take short breaks, can help improve your concentration and efficiency.

4. Eliminate Distractions: Identify and eliminate distractions that hinder your productivity. Turn off notifications on your phone, create a designated workspace, and communicate your need for uninterrupted time to those around you.

5. Practice Mindfulness: Incorporate mindfulness practices into your daily routine. Meditation, deep breathing exercises, and being fully present in the moment can help calm your mind, increase focus, and boost productivity.

6. Break Tasks into Smaller Steps: Large tasks can be overwhelming, leading to procrastination. Break them down into smaller, manageable steps. This approach will make the task seem more achievable and provide a sense of progress as you complete each step.

7. Develop a Routine: Establishing a daily routine helps create structure and consistency. Plan your day by allocating specific time slots for different activities, including work, breaks, exercise, and leisure. Having a routine reduces decision fatigue and ensures that important tasks are regularly attended to.

8. Continuous Learning: Cultivate a thirst for knowledge and personal growth. Invest time in learning new skills, staying updated in your field, and seeking opportunities to expand your knowledge. Continuous learning enhances your productivity by keeping you ahead of the curve.

By implementing these productivity habits into your life, you will experience a profound transformation in your ability to accomplish tasks efficiently and effectively. Remember, productivity is not just about getting more done; it's about creating a fulfilling and joyful existence by finding balance and purpose in your daily activities. Start small, be consistent, and watch as your productivity soars, leading to a happier and more fulfilled life.

Chapter 5: Emotional Intelligence and Relationships

Understanding Emotional Intelligence

Emotional intelligence is the key to living a happy and fulfilled life. In today's fast-paced world, it is imperative that we not only develop our intellectual abilities but also nurture our emotional well-being. This subchapter aims to provide an in-depth understanding of emotional intelligence and its significance in leading a joyful existence.

Emotional intelligence refers to the ability to recognize, understand, and manage our own emotions, as well as effectively navigate and respond to the emotions of others. It encompasses self-awareness, self-regulation, empathy, and social skills. While IQ measures intellectual capacity, emotional intelligence measures our ability to handle relationships, communicate effectively, and make wise decisions.

Developing emotional intelligence is crucial because it allows us to have better control over our emotions and reactions. By being self-aware, we can identify our own emotional triggers and learn to manage them effectively. This self-regulation enables us to respond thoughtfully rather than reacting impulsively in challenging situations.

Empathy, another key aspect of emotional intelligence, allows us to understand and share the feelings of others. By putting ourselves in someone else's shoes, we can build stronger and more meaningful relationships. Empathy fosters compassion, understanding, and open communication, creating an environment conducive to happiness and personal growth.

Furthermore, emotional intelligence plays a significant role in developing social skills. Effective communication, conflict resolution, and collaboration are all essential components of emotional intelligence. By honing these skills, we can establish healthier and more fulfilling relationships, both personally and professionally.

In today's society, where stress, anxiety, and mental health issues are prevalent, emotional intelligence acts as a shield. Enhancing our emotional intelligence equips us with the tools to manage stress, cope with adversity, and maintain a positive mindset. It helps us understand that emotions are natural and that we have the power to choose how to respond to them.

To cultivate emotional intelligence, we must start by becoming more self-aware. This involves recognizing our emotions, understanding their triggers, and accepting them without judgment. From there, we can work on self-regulation, empathy, and improving our social skills through practice and mindfulness.

In conclusion, understanding emotional intelligence is paramount to living a joyful existence. By developing emotional intelligence, we can enhance our self-awareness, manage our emotions effectively, build stronger relationships, and navigate life's challenges with grace. It is a lifelong journey, but one that leads to a happier, more fulfilled life.

Enhancing Emotional Awareness

In the pursuit of a happy life, it is crucial to develop emotional awareness, a skill that empowers individuals to understand and manage their emotions effectively. In this subchapter, we will delve into the significance of enhancing emotional awareness and explore strategies to cultivate this invaluable trait.

Emotional awareness involves recognizing and understanding our own emotions, as well as being attuned to the emotions of others. By developing this skill, we can navigate life's challenges with greater ease, build stronger relationships, and experience a more joyful existence.

To begin enhancing emotional awareness, it is vital to practice self-reflection. Take time each day to check in with yourself and identify how you are feeling. Are you experiencing happiness, sadness, anger, or perhaps a mix of emotions? By acknowledging and accepting our emotions, we can better understand their sources and address them appropriately.

Another powerful technique for enhancing emotional awareness is mindfulness. By being fully present in the moment, we can observe our emotions without judgment. Mindfulness allows us to stay connected to our feelings, helping us gain insights into our thoughts, actions, and reactions. Regular mindfulness practice, such as meditation or deep breathing exercises, can significantly contribute to emotional well-being.

Furthermore, developing empathy plays a vital role in enhancing emotional awareness. Empathy involves putting ourselves in someone else's shoes and understanding their emotions. By actively listening and seeking to understand others, we can build deeper connections and foster harmonious relationships. Practicing empathy not only benefits our personal growth but also contributes to creating a more compassionate and supportive community.

Lastly, journaling can be a powerful tool for enhancing emotional awareness. By writing down our thoughts and feelings, we can gain clarity and identify patterns in our emotions. Journaling provides a safe space to explore and express our emotions, helping us develop a deeper understanding of ourselves.

In conclusion, enhancing emotional awareness is essential for leading a happy life. By developing this skill, we can navigate life's ups and downs with greater resilience, form meaningful connections with others, and experience a more profound sense of joy and fulfillment. Through self-reflection, mindfulness, empathy, and journaling, we can cultivate emotional awareness and embark on a journey of personal growth and self-discovery. Let us embrace this transformative skill and liberate our lives for a more joyful existence.

Effective Communication Skills

Communication is a fundamental aspect of our everyday lives. It is the cornerstone of building and maintaining relationships, resolving conflicts, and expressing our thoughts and emotions. In order to live a happy and fulfilling life, it is crucial to develop effective communication skills. This subchapter explores various strategies and techniques that can help you enhance your communication abilities and foster better relationships.

First and foremost, active listening is a key component of effective communication. It involves fully engaging with the speaker, showing genuine interest, and providing feedback. By actively listening, you not only understand the speaker's message but also validate their feelings and experiences. This fosters a sense of trust and understanding, leading to more meaningful connections.

Furthermore, effective communication requires clarity and conciseness. Being able to articulate your thoughts and ideas in a concise manner ensures that your message is easily understood. It is important to use clear and simple language, avoiding jargon or complicated terms that may confuse the listener. Additionally, non-verbal communication, such as body language and facial expressions, can greatly enhance the clarity of your message.

Empathy is another crucial aspect of effective communication. By putting yourself in the shoes of others and trying to understand their perspective, you can better connect with them on an emotional level. Empathy allows you to respond in a compassionate and understanding manner, creating a safe space for open and honest communication.

In addition, effective communication involves the ability to manage conflicts and disagreements in a constructive manner. Rather than resorting to aggression or passive-aggressiveness, it is important to express your concerns and opinions assertively, while still being respectful of others' viewpoints. This promotes open dialogue and encourages finding mutually beneficial solutions.

Lastly, practicing effective communication skills includes being mindful of your own emotions and reactions. It is essential to manage your emotions and avoid reacting impulsively during conversations. By staying calm and composed, you can express yourself more effectively and prevent misunderstandings or unnecessary conflicts.

In conclusion, effective communication skills are vital for living a happy and fulfilling life. By actively listening, practicing clarity and conciseness, displaying empathy, managing conflicts constructively, and being mindful of your emotions, you can enhance your communication abilities and build stronger and more meaningful relationships. By cultivating these skills, you empower yourself to liberate your life and embrace personal development for a joyful existence.

Building and Maintaining Healthy Relationships

In our journey towards a happy and fulfilling life, one element that plays a crucial role is the quality of our relationships. Whether it's our relationships with family, friends, romantic partners, or even colleagues, these connections can greatly impact our overall well-being. This subchapter aims to provide valuable insights and practical strategies for building and maintaining healthy relationships, ultimately contributing to a joyful existence.

First and foremost, it's important to understand that healthy relationships require effort from both parties involved. Communication is the cornerstone of any successful relationship. Active listening, empathy, and open dialogue are essential to foster understanding and resolve conflicts effectively. By expressing our thoughts and feelings honestly, we create an environment of trust and mutual respect.

Another key aspect of healthy relationships is setting boundaries. It's vital to establish clear limits in order to maintain a healthy balance between giving and receiving. Boundaries help us protect our emotional and physical well-being, while also respecting the boundaries of others. Learning to say "no" when necessary and advocating for ourselves strengthens the foundation of any relationship.

Additionally, cultivating compassion and kindness towards others is vital for nurturing healthy connections. Empathy allows us to better understand the perspectives and emotions of those around us, fostering deeper connections and fostering a harmonious environment. Small acts of kindness can go a long way in strengthening relationships and creating a positive atmosphere.

Forgiveness is another crucial element in building and maintaining healthy relationships. Holding onto grudges and past hurts only hinders growth and creates barriers to genuine connection. By practicing forgiveness, we free ourselves from negative emotions and open up the possibility for healing and stronger bonds.

Lastly, it's important to invest time and effort in nurturing our relationships. Regularly spending quality time with loved ones, expressing appreciation, and supporting each other's goals and aspirations are all essential. By actively participating in each other's lives, we create a sense of belonging and fulfillment that contributes to a happy life.

In conclusion, building and maintaining healthy relationships is a fundamental component of a joyful existence. By fostering open communication, setting boundaries, practicing compassion, forgiveness, and investing time and effort, we can cultivate meaningful connections that enrich our lives. Let us embark on this journey of building healthy relationships, and watch as our happiness and fulfillment soar to new heights.

Chapter 6: Managing Stress and Overcoming Obstacles

Identifying Sources of Stress

In our fast-paced and demanding world, stress has become an inevitable part of our lives. It affects people from all walks of life and can have a significant impact on our overall well-being and happiness. To live a truly joyful existence, it is crucial to identify and address the sources of stress that may be hindering our happiness.

One of the primary steps towards managing stress is recognizing its sources. Stress can arise from various aspects of our lives, and understanding these triggers is essential for effectively tackling them. Let's explore some common sources of stress and how they can impact our pursuit of a happy life.

Work-related stress is a significant contributor to overall stress levels. Long working hours, a heavy workload, unrealistic deadlines, and a lack of work-life balance can leave us feeling overwhelmed and exhausted. Identifying these factors and finding ways to manage them, such as setting boundaries and prioritizing self-care, can greatly alleviate work-related stress.

Personal relationships can also be a source of stress. Difficulties in communication, conflicts, or toxic relationships can all take a toll on our mental and emotional well-being. Taking the time to evaluate our relationships, setting healthy boundaries, and seeking support when needed can help reduce stress in this area.

Financial pressures can be another significant stressor in our lives. Whether it's mounting debt, job insecurity, or the struggle to make ends meet, financial stress can negatively impact our happiness. Creating a budget, seeking financial advice, and developing healthy spending habits can ease the burden of financial stress and bring us closer to a happy and worry-free life.

Health-related stress is often overlooked but can be profoundly impactful. Chronic illnesses, physical pain, or even the fear of developing health issues can cause significant stress. Prioritizing self-care, maintaining a healthy lifestyle, and seeking appropriate medical attention can minimize health-related stress and improve our overall well-being.

Other sources of stress may include major life changes, such as moving, divorce, or loss of a loved one, as well as internal factors like perfectionism or a lack of self-confidence. Recognizing these sources and implementing strategies to cope with them, such as seeking support from loved ones or practicing self-compassion, can help us navigate these challenges and maintain a happier life.

In conclusion, identifying the sources of stress in our lives is a crucial step towards achieving a joyful existence. By recognizing and addressing these triggers, such as work-related stress, personal relationship challenges, financial pressures, health concerns, or major life changes, we can actively work towards reducing stress and fostering a happier life. Remember, you have the power to liberate yourself from stress and create a life filled with joy and fulfillment.

Stress Management Techniques

In today's fast-paced and demanding world, stress has become an inevitable part of our lives. Whether it is due to work pressures, relationship issues, or financial concerns, stress can take a toll on our mental and physical well-being. However, there are effective stress management techniques that can help us regain control and lead a happier life.

1. Deep Breathing: One of the simplest yet most powerful techniques to manage stress is deep breathing. By taking slow, deep breaths, we activate the body's relaxation response, triggering a calming effect on our mind and body. Practice deep breathing exercises whenever you feel stressed or overwhelmed.

2. Exercise: Engaging in regular physical activity is not only beneficial for our physical health but also plays a crucial role in managing stress. Exercise releases endorphins, which are natural mood-enhancers, and helps reduce cortisol, the stress hormone. Find an activity you enjoy, whether it's jogging, dancing, or practicing yoga, and make it a part of your routine.

3. Mindfulness Meditation: Mindfulness meditation is a powerful technique that helps us stay present and focused on the current moment. It involves observing our thoughts and emotions without judgment. By practicing mindfulness, we can develop a greater sense of self-awareness and detach ourselves from unnecessary stressors.

4. Time Management: Poor time management often leads to excessive stress. Learning to prioritize tasks, set realistic goals, and delegate when necessary can significantly reduce stress levels. Make a to-do list,

break tasks into smaller, manageable chunks, and avoid multitasking to enhance productivity and decrease stress.

5. Social Support: Building a strong support system is vital for managing stress and leading a happy life. Surround yourself with positive, supportive individuals who can provide guidance and emotional comfort when needed. Sharing your concerns and seeking advice from trusted friends or family members can help alleviate stress.

6. Self-Care: Taking care of yourself is crucial for maintaining a happy and stress-free life. Engage in activities that bring you joy and relaxation, such as reading a book, taking a long bath, pursuing a hobby, or spending time in nature. Prioritize self-care and make it a non-negotiable part of your routine.

Remember, stress is a natural part of life, but how we choose to respond to it is within our control. By incorporating these stress management techniques into your daily life, you can regain balance, reduce stress levels, and embrace a joyful existence.

Developing Resilience in the Face of Challenges

Subchapter: Developing Resilience in the Face of Challenges

Introduction

Life is a beautiful journey, but it is not without its share of challenges. We all face obstacles and setbacks that can make us question our abilities and undermine our happiness. However, the key to living a truly joyful existence lies in developing resilience - the ability to bounce back stronger and wiser from life's trials. In this subchapter, we will explore how to cultivate resilience and overcome challenges, ultimately leading to a happier and more fulfilling life.

1. Embrace Change as an Opportunity

Life is constantly changing, and the more we resist it, the harder it becomes to find happiness. By embracing change as an opportunity for growth, we unlock our potential to adapt and thrive. Cultivate a mindset that sees challenges as stepping stones towards personal development and self-improvement.

2. Cultivate a Supportive Network

We are all stronger when we have a support system to lean on during tough times. Surround yourself with positive and uplifting individuals who believe in your abilities. Share your challenges with them, seek their guidance, and draw strength from their experiences. Remember, you don't have to face challenges alone.

3. Develop Emotional Intelligence

Emotional intelligence is the ability to understand and manage our own emotions and effectively navigate the emotions of others. By developing emotional intelligence, we can respond to challenges with resilience and grace. Practice self-awareness, empathy, and emotional regulation to build a solid foundation for facing any obstacles that come your way.

4. Embrace Failure as a Learning Opportunity

Failure is not the end; it is a valuable teacher. Instead of being discouraged by setbacks, embrace them as opportunities for growth and learning. Analyze your failures, identify the lessons they offer, and use them to refine your strategies. With each failure, you move closer to success.

5. Practice Self-Care

Resilience requires a strong foundation, and that foundation begins with taking care of ourselves. Prioritize self-care by engaging in activities that bring you joy, practicing mindfulness and gratitude, and maintaining a healthy lifestyle. When you prioritize your well-being, you build resilience and are better equipped to face any challenges that come your way.

Conclusion

Developing resilience in the face of challenges is crucial for creating a happy life. By embracing change, cultivating a supportive network, developing emotional intelligence, embracing failure as a learning opportunity, and practicing self-care, you can build the resilience needed to overcome any obstacle. Remember, challenges are merely opportunities for growth, and with resilience, you can liberate your life and live a joyful existence.

Overcoming Procrastination and Self-Doubt

Procrastination and self-doubt can be two major roadblocks on the path to a happy life. They often go hand in hand, holding us back from reaching our full potential and experiencing a truly joyful existence. In this subchapter, we will explore effective strategies to overcome these obstacles and liberate ourselves from their grip.

Procrastination is a common phenomenon that affects people from all walks of life. It is the act of delaying or avoiding tasks and responsibilities, often resulting in stress, missed opportunities, and a sense of dissatisfaction. To overcome procrastination, it is crucial to understand its root causes. It may be fueled by fear, perfectionism, lack of motivation, or a combination of these factors. By identifying the underlying reasons for procrastination, we can develop tailored strategies to address them.

One powerful approach is to break tasks into smaller, manageable steps. By focusing on one small action at a time, we can alleviate the overwhelming feeling that often leads to procrastination. Setting specific goals with achievable deadlines can also provide a sense of structure and accountability, helping us stay on track.

Self-doubt, on the other hand, stems from a lack of confidence in our abilities and worthiness. It often manifests as negative self-talk and limiting beliefs, sabotaging our efforts to pursue happiness. Overcoming self-doubt requires a shift in mindset and a commitment to self-compassion and self-acceptance.

One effective strategy is to challenge negative thoughts and replace them with positive affirmations. Surrounding ourselves with supportive and uplifting individuals can also boost our confidence and help us overcome self-doubt. Additionally, practicing self-care and engaging in activities that bring us joy and fulfillment can enhance our self-esteem and provide a solid foundation for personal growth.

In conclusion, overcoming procrastination and self-doubt is crucial for cultivating a happy life. By implementing strategies such as breaking tasks into manageable steps, setting goals, challenging negative thoughts, and practicing self-care, we can break free from the shackles of procrastination and self-doubt. Remember, you have the power to liberate yourself from these obstacles and create a joyful existence filled with purpose and fulfillment. Start today and embrace the journey towards a happier life.

Chapter 7: Cultivating a Meaningful Life

Discovering Your Life Purpose

Chapter 4: Discovering Your Life Purpose

In this subchapter, we will embark on a journey of self-discovery to help you uncover your life purpose. Each one of us has a unique reason for being on this Earth, and understanding our purpose can bring immense joy and fulfillment to our lives. Whether you are seeking a happy life or simply looking for direction, this exploration will guide you towards a more purposeful existence.

1.   Awakening   the   Inner   Self: To discover your life purpose, you must first connect with your inner self. Take the time to reflect on your values, passions, and dreams. What truly makes you happy? What activities do you find yourself drawn to? By delving into your authentic self, you will gain valuable insights that will guide you towards your life purpose.

2.   Uncovering   Your   Gifts: Each individual possesses unique talents and gifts that can be used to fulfill their life purpose. Consider your strengths, skills, and natural abilities. What comes easily to you? What do others often praise you for? By recognizing and cultivating these gifts, you can align them with your life purpose and create a path towards a more joyful existence.

3.   Exploring   Your   Passions: Passions are the driving force behind a happy life. What activities make you lose track of time? What topics or causes ignite a fire within you? By following your passions, you can unlock your true potential

and make a positive impact on the world around you. Your life purpose often lies within the intersection of your gifts, passions, and values.

4.   Embracing   Challenges   and   Growth: Discovering your life purpose is not always a linear journey. It involves embracing challenges, setbacks, and opportunities for growth. Be open to new experiences, step out of your comfort zone, and learn from both successes and failures. These obstacles will shape you into the person you are meant to be and lead you closer to your life purpose.

5.   Taking   Action: Once you have gained clarity on your life purpose, it is essential to take action. Create a plan and set achievable goals that align with your purpose. Surround yourself with a support system that encourages and uplifts you. As you move forward, remember that your life purpose may evolve and change over time. Embrace this growth and adapt accordingly.

Discovering your life purpose is a transformative journey that can lead to a happy and fulfilling existence. By awakening your inner self, uncovering your gifts, exploring your passions, embracing challenges, and taking action, you will be well on your way to living a purpose-driven life. Remember, your life purpose is unique to you, and the world needs your unique contributions. Embrace this opportunity to liberate your life and embark on a joyful existence filled with meaning and purpose.

Setting Meaningful Goals

In order to live a truly happy life, it is essential to set meaningful goals. Goals give us direction, purpose, and a sense of fulfillment. They provide us with the motivation and inspiration to overcome obstacles and make progress towards the life we desire. In this subchapter, we will explore the importance of setting meaningful goals and provide practical strategies for doing so.

Why are meaningful goals important? Well, without goals, we can easily feel lost or stuck in a monotonous routine. Meaningful goals give us something to strive for, something to look forward to. They allow us to envision a better future and take actionable steps towards making it a reality. When we have clear goals, it becomes easier to prioritize our time and energy, making decisions that align with our values and aspirations.

So, how do we set meaningful goals? Firstly, it is important to reflect on what truly matters to us. Take a moment to consider your values, passions, and dreams. What brings you joy? What activities make you feel fulfilled? By identifying these aspects of your life, you can begin to set goals that align with your personal definition of happiness.

Next, it is crucial to make your goals specific and measurable. Vague goals like "be happy" or "live a fulfilling life" are difficult to achieve because they lack clarity. Instead, break your goals down into smaller, actionable steps. For example, if your goal is to improve your physical health, you could set specific targets like exercising for 30 minutes five times a week or eating a balanced diet.

Furthermore, it is essential to set realistic goals. While it is important to challenge yourself, setting unattainable goals can lead to frustration and disappointment. Start with small, achievable goals and gradually increase the difficulty as you gain confidence and make progress.

Finally, it is crucial to regularly review and revise your goals. Life is fluid, and our priorities and aspirations may change over time. By regularly reassessing your goals, you can ensure they remain meaningful and relevant to your current circumstances.

In conclusion, setting meaningful goals is a vital aspect of living a happy life. They provide us with a sense of purpose, motivation, and fulfillment. By reflecting on our values and passions, making goals specific and measurable, setting realistic targets, and regularly reviewing our goals, we can create a roadmap to a more joyful existence. So, take the time to set meaningful goals for yourself and liberate your life from the constraints of uncertainty and aimlessness.

Creating a Vision Board for Inspiration

In our quest for a happy life, it is crucial to find inspiration and clarity in our goals and dreams. One powerful tool that can help us achieve this is a vision board. A vision board is a visual representation of our aspirations, desires, and dreams that serves as a constant reminder of what we want to achieve in life. It is a powerful tool that can help us manifest our dreams into reality.

To create a vision board, start by setting aside some dedicated time and space. Gather materials such as a poster board, magazines, scissors, glue, and markers. Find a quiet and comfortable place where you can focus without distractions. Begin by reflecting on what truly makes you happy and what you want to achieve in your life. This could be anything from career aspirations, personal relationships, health and fitness goals, or even travel adventures.

Once you have a clear understanding of your desires, start flipping through magazines and cutting out images and words that resonate with your dreams. Don't limit yourself to just one area; explore different aspects of your life that contribute to your overall happiness. Whether it's a picture of a tropical beach or a motivational quote, choose visuals that evoke positive emotions and inspire you.

Next, arrange the cut-outs on the poster board in a way that feels natural to you. You could organize them by categories or create a collage of images that represent your entire vision. Be creative and allow your intuition to guide you. Once you are satisfied with the arrangement, glue the cut-outs onto the board.

Now that your vision board is complete, find a prominent place to display it where you will see it every day. It could be your bedroom wall, office desk, or any other place that you frequent. Take a few minutes each day to look at your vision board and visualize yourself achieving those dreams. By consistently focusing on your vision, you are sending a clear message to the universe about your intentions and desires.

Remember, a vision board is not a magical solution that guarantees instant success. It is a tool that helps you stay focused and motivated on your journey towards a happy life. Embrace the process and be open to new opportunities that align with your vision. As you take inspired action and make progress towards your goals, your vision board will serve as a constant reminder of the life you are creating for yourself.

In conclusion, creating a vision board is an empowering activity that can bring clarity, inspiration, and joy to your life. It helps you visualize your dreams and stay motivated on your path towards a happy existence. So, embrace your creativity, explore your deepest desires, and start manifesting the life you truly deserve.

Finding Fulfillment in Everyday Life

In our pursuit of happiness, we often overlook the simple joys that can be found in our everyday lives. We are constantly chasing after big achievements, material possessions, or external validation, thinking that these are the keys to a happy life. However, true fulfillment lies not in grand accomplishments, but in finding joy and contentment in the present moment.

To begin the journey of finding fulfillment in everyday life, it is essential to cultivate a mindset of gratitude. Taking a moment each day to appreciate the blessings we have, no matter how small, can shift our focus from what is lacking to what is already abundant in our lives. Whether it is a sunny day, a delicious meal, or the company of loved ones, these simple pleasures can bring immense happiness if we allow ourselves to acknowledge and savor them.

Another aspect of finding fulfillment is learning to live mindfully. Often, we are so caught up in our thoughts about the past or worries about the future that we fail to fully experience the present moment. By practicing mindfulness, we can bring our attention to the here and now, fully immersing ourselves in whatever we are doing. Whether it is sipping a cup of tea, going for a walk, or engaging in a conversation, being fully present allows us to find joy in the simplest of activities.

Moreover, finding fulfillment in everyday life involves aligning our actions with our values and passions. It is important to identify what truly brings us joy and purpose, and actively pursue those activities, hobbies, or causes. Engaging in activities that resonate with our authentic selves not only brings a sense of fulfillment but also allows us to tap into our unique talents and strengths.

Lastly, finding fulfillment in everyday life requires nurturing our relationships. Human connection and meaningful relationships are vital for our happiness and well-being. Taking the time to connect with loved ones, expressing gratitude, and offering acts of kindness can bring immense fulfillment and deepen our sense of belonging.

In conclusion, finding fulfillment in everyday life is not about waiting for extraordinary moments; it is about embracing the ordinary moments and finding the extraordinary within them. By cultivating gratitude, living mindfully, pursuing our passions, and nurturing relationships, we can unlock the abundant joy and fulfillment that lie within the fabric of our daily lives. So, let us liberate ourselves from the pursuit of external achievements and embrace the beauty and fulfillment that exists in every moment.

Chapter 8: Self-Care and Well-Being

The Importance of Self-Care

In today's fast-paced and demanding world, it is easy to get caught up in the hustle and bustle of daily life and neglect our own well-being. However, taking care of ourselves is not a luxury; it is a necessity. Self-care is the foundation for a happy and fulfilling life, and it is essential for our overall well-being.

Self-care encompasses all the actions we take to nurture our physical, mental, and emotional health. It involves making choices that prioritize our well-being and ensure that we are functioning at our best. By practicing self-care, we can prevent burnout, reduce stress, and increase our happiness and satisfaction in life.

One of the key aspects of self-care is taking care of our physical health. This includes getting enough sleep, eating a balanced diet, and engaging in regular exercise. When we prioritize our physical well-being, we have more energy, feel better both mentally and emotionally, and are better equipped to handle the challenges that life throws at us.

Another important component of self-care is taking care of our mental and emotional health. This can involve activities such as practicing mindfulness and meditation, engaging in hobbies and activities that bring us joy, and seeking support from friends, family, or professionals when needed. Taking time to relax and recharge is crucial for our mental and emotional well-being.

Self-care also means setting boundaries and learning to say no when necessary. It is okay to prioritize our own needs and say no to things that do not serve us or make us happy. By setting boundaries and learning to say no, we can avoid overcommitting ourselves and feeling overwhelmed.

In essence, self-care is an act of self-love and self-respect. It is about taking responsibility for our own well-being and making choices that prioritize our happiness and fulfillment. By practicing self-care, we can cultivate a joyful existence and lead a happier, more balanced life.

Remember, self-care is not selfish; it is essential. Take the time to nurture yourself and prioritize your well-being. You deserve it, and the benefits will ripple out into all areas of your life. Embrace self-care as a way to liberate yourself and create a truly joyful existence.

Nurturing Your Physical Health

In the pursuit of a happy life, it is crucial to recognize the importance of nurturing your physical health. Our bodies are the vessels that carry us through life, and by prioritizing our physical well-being, we can lay a solid foundation for a joyful existence. This subchapter aims to provide you with valuable strategies and insights to help you cultivate and maintain optimal physical health.

Regular exercise is a cornerstone of physical well-being. Engaging in physical activity not only helps to keep your body fit and strong but also boosts your mood and overall mental well-being. Find activities that you enjoy, whether it's going for a brisk walk, attending a dance class, or practicing yoga. Incorporate these activities into your daily routine, making them a non-negotiable part of your day.

Another essential aspect of nurturing your physical health is maintaining a balanced and nutritious diet. Fueling your body with wholesome, nutrient-rich foods will provide you with the energy and vitality needed to live a fulfilling life. Focus on incorporating a variety of fruits, vegetables, whole grains, lean proteins, and healthy fats into your diet. Stay hydrated by drinking plenty of water throughout the day.

Prioritize getting enough sleep each night. Sleep is a vital component of physical and mental well-being. Aim for seven to eight hours of uninterrupted sleep to allow your body to repair and rejuvenate itself. Establish a relaxing bedtime routine and create a comfortable sleep environment to enhance the quality of your rest.

Regular check-ups with healthcare professionals are crucial for maintaining your physical health. Schedule regular visits with your doctor, dentist, and optometrist to ensure that any potential health issues are detected and addressed early on. Prevention is always better than cure, and these check-ups play a vital role in taking proactive care of your well-being.

Lastly, listen to your body and practice self-care. Pay attention to any signs of discomfort or pain and take appropriate action. Engage in activities that bring you joy and help you unwind, such as taking relaxing baths, practicing meditation, or spending time in nature. Remember that your physical health is intrinsically connected to your overall happiness and well-being.

By nurturing your physical health, you are investing in yourself and creating a solid foundation for a joyful existence. Prioritize exercise, maintain a balanced diet, get enough sleep, schedule regular check-ups, and practice self-care. By doing so, you will pave the way towards a healthier, happier life.

Prioritizing Mental and Emotional Well-Being

In our fast-paced, demanding world, it's easy to get caught up in the whirlwind of responsibilities and forget about our own mental and emotional well-being. However, in order to truly live a happy and fulfilled life, it is essential to prioritize our mental and emotional health. This subchapter will delve into the strategies and techniques that can help you achieve a joyful existence by nurturing your internal well-being.

First and foremost, it is crucial to recognize the importance of self-care. Taking the time to engage in activities that bring you joy, peace, and relaxation can do wonders for your mental and emotional state. Whether it's practicing mindfulness and meditation, indulging in a hobby, or simply spending quality time with loved ones, make self-care a non-negotiable part of your routine.

Another key aspect of prioritizing mental and emotional well-being is maintaining healthy relationships. Surrounding yourself with positive, supportive individuals who uplift and inspire you is essential for a happy life. Cultivating meaningful connections and open communication can significantly contribute to your overall well-being and bring a sense of belonging and fulfillment.

Furthermore, it is crucial to develop effective coping mechanisms to handle stress and adversity. Life is full of challenges, and it is how we respond to them that determines our mental and emotional well-being. Learning healthy ways to manage stress, such as exercise, journaling, or seeking professional help when needed, can make a world of difference in your happiness and mental clarity.

In addition, practicing gratitude and cultivating a positive mindset are essential components of prioritizing mental and emotional well-being. Taking time each day to reflect on the things you are grateful for can shift your perspective and bring a sense of contentment. By focusing on the positives in your life, you can develop resilience and find joy even in the face of difficulties.

Lastly, remember that self-compassion is vital. Treat yourself with kindness, understanding, and forgiveness. Embrace your imperfections and understand that it is okay to make mistakes. Being gentle with yourself and practicing self-acceptance can contribute greatly to your mental and emotional well-being.

In conclusion, prioritizing mental and emotional well-being is crucial for living a happy and fulfilling life. By incorporating self-care, maintaining healthy relationships, developing effective coping mechanisms, practicing gratitude, and cultivating self-compassion, you can liberate yourself from the burden of stress and achieve a joyful existence. Take the time to invest in your internal well-being, and you will reap the rewards of a happier and more fulfilling life.

Incorporating Mindfulness and Meditation Practices

In today's fast-paced and chaotic world, finding inner peace and happiness can often feel like a distant dream. We are constantly bombarded with stressors and distractions that pull us away from the present moment, leaving us feeling overwhelmed and disconnected. However, there is a powerful tool that can help us navigate the challenges of life and cultivate a joyful existence – mindfulness and meditation practices.

Mindfulness is the practice of being fully present and aware of our thoughts, feelings, and sensations without judgment. By training our minds to focus on the present moment, we can break free from the grip of anxiety and worry, and instead, embrace a sense of calm and clarity. Through mindfulness, we can learn to appreciate the simple pleasures of life, enhance our relationships, and develop a greater understanding of ourselves.

One of the most effective ways to cultivate mindfulness is through meditation. Meditation allows us to quiet the mind and connect with our inner selves. By dedicating a few minutes each day to sit in stillness and observe our thoughts, we can gradually train our minds to let go of negative patterns and embrace a more positive outlook on life. Scientific research has shown that regular meditation practice can reduce stress, improve focus, enhance emotional well-being, and even boost our immune system.

Incorporating mindfulness and meditation into our daily lives doesn't require a significant time commitment or any special equipment. It can be as simple as taking a few deep breaths and bringing our attention to the sensations in our bodies, or setting aside a few minutes each morning to sit quietly and observe our thoughts. The key is to approach these practices with an open mind and a willingness to explore our inner world.

By incorporating mindfulness and meditation practices into our lives, we can unlock the secret to a happy and fulfilling existence. These practices offer us a path to liberation from the stresses and worries that hold us back, and empower us to live with intention and purpose. Whether we are seeking to find inner peace, improve our relationships, or enhance our overall well-being, mindfulness and meditation are invaluable tools that can transform our lives. Embrace these practices, and let them guide you on a journey towards a joyful existence.

Chapter 9: Enhancing Personal Growth Through Learning

The Lifelong Learning Mindset

In the pursuit of a happy life, one of the most crucial aspects to embrace is the lifelong learning mindset. This mindset involves a continuous desire to expand our knowledge, skills, and personal growth throughout our entire existence. It is a powerful tool that can transform our lives, allowing us to unlock our full potential and find joy in the process.

In today's rapidly changing world, the importance of lifelong learning cannot be overstated. The knowledge and skills we acquired in our early years may no longer be sufficient to navigate the challenges and opportunities that arise in our personal and professional lives. By adopting a lifelong learning mindset, we open ourselves up to new possibilities, constantly adapting and evolving to meet the ever-changing demands of life.

One of the key benefits of the lifelong learning mindset is its ability to keep our minds sharp and active. As we challenge ourselves to learn new things, whether it's a new language, a musical instrument, or a new hobby, we stimulate our brain and keep it engaged. This not only enhances our cognitive abilities but also improves our memory, creativity, and problem-solving skills.

Moreover, the lifelong learning mindset encourages us to step out of our comfort zones and embrace new experiences. It enables us to see the world from different perspectives, fostering empathy and understanding. By continuously learning and exploring, we expand our horizons and become more open-minded individuals, capable of embracing diversity and finding joy in the richness of life.

Additionally, lifelong learning allows us to stay relevant in an ever-evolving world. With the rapid advancement of technology and the changing job market, acquiring new skills and knowledge is crucial for career growth and personal development. By staying curious and continuously seeking knowledge, we ensure that we remain adaptable and resilient in the face of change.

Ultimately, the lifelong learning mindset is a powerful catalyst for personal growth, fulfillment, and a joyful existence. It encourages us to embrace every opportunity as a chance to learn and grow, whether it's a success or a failure. It reminds us that the journey is just as important as the destination and that our potential for growth and happiness is limitless.

So, let us embrace the lifelong learning mindset and liberate our lives from stagnation and complacency. Let us commit to being perpetual students of life, always seeking new knowledge, skills, and experiences. By doing so, we can unlock our true potential and create a life filled with joy, fulfillment, and endless possibilities.

Expanding Your Knowledge and Skills

In the pursuit of a happy life, personal growth and continuous learning play a pivotal role. Our journey towards a joyful existence is not limited to external factors but heavily relies on our ability to expand our knowledge and skills. This subchapter aims to enlighten and empower individuals from all walks of life, emphasizing the importance of lifelong learning and personal development.

Learning is a lifelong process that goes beyond the walls of classrooms and formal education. It is about embracing curiosity, seeking new experiences, and challenging ourselves to become better versions of who we are. When we actively engage in expanding our knowledge and skills, we open doors to endless possibilities and uncover hidden talents we never knew we possessed.

One of the key benefits of expanding our knowledge and skills is personal growth. Through learning, we gain a deeper understanding of ourselves, our values, and our purpose. We discover new passions, interests, and strengths that contribute to our overall happiness and fulfillment. Whether it's learning a new language, mastering a musical instrument, or acquiring professional certifications, each new skill acquired adds depth and richness to our lives, making them more vibrant and enjoyable.

Moreover, expanding our knowledge and skills fosters adaptability and resilience in the face of life's challenges. The world is constantly evolving, and the ability to stay relevant and keep up with changes is essential for a happy life. By embracing a growth mindset, we become more open to new ideas, perspectives, and opportunities, allowing us to navigate obstacles with confidence and grace.

Expanding our knowledge and skills also enables us to make meaningful contributions to society. As we become more knowledgeable and skilled in our areas of interest, we can share our expertise and talents with others, positively impacting their lives. Whether it's mentoring, volunteering, or teaching, our newfound knowledge becomes a catalyst for collective growth and happiness.

In conclusion, expanding our knowledge and skills is a transformative journey that leads to a truly joyful existence. By embracing lifelong learning and personal development, we unlock our full potential, foster personal growth, and contribute to the well-being of society. So, let us embark on this journey together, with an open mind and a thirst for knowledge, as we liberate our lives and create a future filled with happiness and fulfillment.

Seeking Personal Growth Opportunities

In our quest for a happy and fulfilling life, it is crucial to recognize the importance of personal growth. Personal growth is the ongoing process of self-improvement, self-discovery, and self-actualization. It involves developing new skills, expanding our knowledge, and nurturing our emotional, mental, and spiritual well-being. By actively seeking personal growth opportunities, we can unlock our true potential and live a more joyful existence.

One of the first steps in seeking personal growth opportunities is to cultivate a growth mindset. This mindset acknowledges that our abilities and intelligence are not fixed traits but can be developed through dedication and effort. Embracing a growth mindset allows us to approach challenges and setbacks as learning opportunities, enabling us to persevere and grow stronger in the face of adversity.

To embark on a personal growth journey, it is essential to set clear goals. By identifying what we want to achieve and the areas we want to improve, we can create a roadmap for our personal development. These goals can range from acquiring new skills, such as learning a musical instrument or a foreign language, to improving our emotional intelligence or developing better communication skills. It is important to set SMART goals – specific, measurable, achievable, relevant, and time-bound – to ensure we stay focused and motivated.

Seeking personal growth opportunities also involves stepping out of our comfort zones. Growth occurs when we challenge ourselves and take risks. Whether it is trying a new hobby, taking up a leadership role, or traveling to unfamiliar places, stepping outside our comfort zone allows us to expand our horizons, gain new experiences, and discover hidden talents.

Furthermore, seeking personal growth opportunities requires a commitment to lifelong learning. We should never stop acquiring knowledge and seeking new experiences. Reading books, attending workshops, taking online courses, or engaging in meaningful conversations with others can all contribute to our personal growth. By continuously learning and exposing ourselves to new ideas and perspectives, we can broaden our understanding of the world and evolve as individuals.

Lastly, seeking personal growth opportunities involves self-reflection and introspection. Taking the time to evaluate our strengths, weaknesses, and values allows us to gain clarity about who we are and what truly matters to us. Through practices such as meditation, journaling, or seeking guidance from mentors or therapists, we can gain insights into ourselves and make conscious decisions that align with our authentic selves.

In conclusion, seeking personal growth opportunities is essential for a happy life. By cultivating a growth mindset, setting clear goals, stepping out of our comfort zones, committing to lifelong learning, and engaging in self-reflection, we can unlock our true potential and live a more fulfilling existence. Embrace personal growth as a lifelong journey, and liberate your life from limitations.

Embracing Challenges and Continuous Improvement

In our quest for a truly happy life, we must be willing to embrace challenges and commit to continuous improvement. Life is full of obstacles and setbacks, but it is how we respond to them that determines our level of happiness and personal growth.

Challenges are not meant to break us; they are opportunities for growth and self-discovery. By facing challenges head-on, we push ourselves outside our comfort zones and unlock our true potential. It is during these moments of adversity that we learn the most about ourselves and our capabilities. Instead of shying away from challenges, we should see them as stepping stones to a more fulfilling and joyful existence.

Continuous improvement is the key to personal development and lasting happiness. We should always strive to be better versions of ourselves, constantly seeking ways to grow and evolve. This could mean learning new skills, pursuing further education, or simply adopting a mindset of curiosity and self-reflection. By committing to continuous improvement, we open ourselves up to endless possibilities and experiences, enriching our lives in ways we never thought possible.

Embracing challenges and continuously improving requires a shift in mindset. We must adopt a positive outlook and believe in our ability to overcome any obstacle that comes our way. Challenges are not roadblocks but opportunities for personal transformation. By reframing our perception of challenges, we can approach them with a sense of excitement and curiosity, knowing that they hold the potential to propel us towards a happier and more fulfilling life.

It is important to remember that embracing challenges and continuous improvement is not a one-time endeavor but a lifelong commitment. The journey towards personal growth is ongoing, and as we overcome one challenge, another will inevitably present itself. It is through this process of continuous improvement that we find true happiness, as we are constantly evolving and becoming the best versions of ourselves.

So, let us embrace challenges with open arms and commit to continuous improvement. Let us view challenges as opportunities for growth and personal development, knowing that they are essential in our pursuit of a joyful existence. By embracing challenges and continuously improving, we unlock our full potential and create a life filled with happiness, fulfillment, and personal success.

Chapter 10: Creating a Joyful Existence

Embracing Positivity and Gratitude

In our fast-paced and often chaotic world, it's easy to get caught up in the negative aspects of life. We often find ourselves focusing on what's wrong, what we don't have, or what's not going according to plan. But what if we could shift our perspective and embrace positivity and gratitude instead? What if we could cultivate a happy life by simply changing our mindset?

In this subchapter, "Embracing Positivity and Gratitude," we will explore the transformative power of these two essential elements in creating a joyful existence. Whether you're seeking happiness, fulfillment, or a greater sense of purpose, this is the key to unlocking your potential.

Positivity is not about ignoring or denying life's challenges; rather, it's about choosing to see the silver lining in every situation. By adopting a positive mindset, we can train ourselves to focus on the good, no matter how small or insignificant it may seem. This shift in perspective allows us to approach life with optimism, resilience, and an unwavering belief in our ability to overcome any obstacle.

Gratitude is the practice of acknowledging and appreciating the blessings in our lives. It is the recognition that even in the midst of adversity, there is always something to be thankful for. By cultivating an attitude of gratitude, we can train ourselves to find joy in the simplest of moments – a beautiful sunset, a warm cup of coffee, or the laughter of loved ones. Gratitude not only enhances our overall sense of well-being, but it also fosters deeper connections with others and a greater appreciation for the world around us.

In this subchapter, we will explore practical strategies for incorporating positivity and gratitude into your daily life. From simple exercises like keeping a gratitude journal or practicing positive affirmations, to more profound techniques such as meditation and mindfulness, you will discover a multitude of tools to help you embrace these transformative practices.

Remember, embracing positivity and gratitude is not a one-time event but a lifelong journey. It requires consistent effort and a commitment to retrain our minds to focus on the positive. So, join us on this path towards a happier, more fulfilling existence. Together, let's liberate our lives by embracing the power of positivity and gratitude.

Living in Alignment with Your Values

In our pursuit of happiness, we often find ourselves feeling lost or unfulfilled. We may have achieved success in various aspects of our lives, such as a successful career, a loving relationship, or financial stability, yet still feel a void within us. This void can be attributed to the misalignment between our actions and our core values.

Living in alignment with your values is the key to unlocking a truly happy life. When you live in accordance with your values, you experience a sense of purpose, fulfillment, and inner peace. It allows you to live authentically and make choices that are in line with your true self.

Identifying your core values is the first step towards living in alignment with them. Take a moment to reflect on what truly matters to you. Is it kindness, honesty, family, or personal growth? Write down a list of values that resonate with you and prioritize them based on their importance to you.

Once you have identified your values, it's time to bring them into your daily life. Start by examining your current actions and behaviors. Do they align with your values? Are there any areas of your life where you feel a disconnect? If so, it's time to make changes.

Living in alignment with your values requires conscious decision-making. It means choosing to prioritize what truly matters to you over societal expectations or external pressures. It may involve making difficult choices or stepping out of your comfort zone, but the rewards are immeasurable.

Integrating your values into your daily life can be done in various ways. For example, if one of your core values is health, you can prioritize regular exercise and nourishing your body with wholesome foods. If personal growth is important to you, set aside time for reading, learning, or pursuing hobbies that challenge you.

Living in alignment with your values also means surrounding yourself with people who share similar values. Surrounding yourself with like-minded individuals can provide support, encouragement, and a sense of belonging. Seek out communities, organizations, or groups that align with your values and actively engage with them.

Remember, living in alignment with your values is an ongoing journey. As you grow and evolve, your values may change too. Continuously evaluate and reassess your values to ensure they are still aligned with your true self.

In conclusion, living in alignment with your values is vital for a happy life. It brings a sense of purpose, fulfillment, and inner peace. Identify your core values, integrate them into your daily life, and surround yourself with like-minded individuals. Embrace this journey of self-discovery, and watch as your life transforms into a joyful existence.

Celebrating Your Achievements

Subchapter: Celebrating Your Achievements

Introduction:
In our journey towards a happy life, it is essential to acknowledge and celebrate our achievements. Too often, we get caught up in the pursuit of our goals and forget to take a moment to appreciate how far we have come. Celebrating achievements not only boosts our self-esteem but also fuels our motivation to continue striving for success. In this subchapter, we will explore the importance of celebrating achievements and discover ways to honor our progress on the path to a joyful existence.

Recognizing Your Progress:
One of the key elements of celebrating achievements is recognizing the progress you have made. Take a step back and reflect on the small milestones you have achieved on your journey. Perhaps you have reached a fitness goal, completed a challenging project, or made significant strides in personal growth. Recognizing these achievements, no matter how small, reinforces the belief that you are capable of accomplishing great things.

Expressing Gratitude:
Celebrating achievements goes hand in hand with expressing gratitude. Gratitude allows us to cultivate a positive mindset and appreciate the blessings in our lives. Take the time to express gratitude for the opportunities that have led to your achievements. This can be done through simple acts such as journaling, writing thank-you notes, or sharing your gratitude with loved ones. By acknowledging the support you have received along the way, you not only honor your achievements but also strengthen your relationships.

Rewarding   Yourself:
Rewarding yourself is a powerful way to celebrate your achievements and motivate yourself to reach new heights. Treat yourself to something you enjoy, whether it's a relaxing spa day, a weekend getaway, or indulging in your favorite meal. By consciously acknowledging your accomplishments and rewarding yourself, you reinforce positive behaviors and create a sense of fulfillment.

Sharing   Your   Success:
Sharing your success with others can be incredibly rewarding. By sharing your achievements, you inspire others to pursue their own goals and create a ripple effect of positivity. Whether it's through social media, a blog, or a simple conversation, be proud of your accomplishments and share your journey with others. By doing so, you not only celebrate your achievements but also become a source of inspiration and motivation for others.

Conclusion:
In the pursuit of a happy life, celebrating your achievements is essential. Recognize your progress, express gratitude, reward yourself, and share your success with others. By embracing and celebrating your achievements, you cultivate a positive mindset, boost your self-esteem, and fuel your motivation to continue growing and evolving on your journey towards a joyful existence. Take a moment today to celebrate how far you have come, and let it propel you towards even greater accomplishments.

Spreading Joy and Kindness to Others

In our fast-paced and often chaotic world, it is easy to get caught up in our own lives, focusing solely on our own happiness and success. However, true happiness lies in the ability to spread joy and kindness to others. When we make the conscious effort to brighten someone else's day, we not only bring happiness to their lives but also experience a profound sense of fulfillment and purpose in our own.

Spreading joy and kindness is a simple yet powerful concept that can transform our lives and the lives of those around us. It begins with small acts of kindness, such as offering a genuine smile to a stranger, holding the door for someone, or simply saying "thank you" to those who serve us. These seemingly insignificant gestures can have a ripple effect, creating a positive chain reaction that spreads happiness to others.

One of the most effective ways to spread joy is through acts of service. Volunteering our time and skills to help those in need not only makes a difference in their lives but also allows us to connect with our own humanity. Whether it's donating to a local charity, participating in community projects, or lending a helping hand to a friend or neighbor, acts of service remind us of the inherent goodness within all of us.

Additionally, spreading joy and kindness involves practicing empathy and understanding. Taking the time to truly listen to others, offering a shoulder to lean on, or providing words of encouragement can make a significant impact on someone's emotional well-being. By demonstrating compassion and empathy, we create a safe space for others to express their thoughts and feelings, fostering deeper connections and stronger relationships.

Furthermore, acts of generosity can bring immense joy to both the giver and the receiver. Whether it's sharing our resources, giving heartfelt compliments, or surprising someone with a small gift, generosity opens our hearts and reminds us of the abundance in our lives. It allows us to shift our focus from scarcity to abundance, attracting more positivity and happiness into our own lives.

Spreading joy and kindness to others is not only beneficial for the recipients but also for ourselves. It creates a sense of interconnectedness and reminds us that we are all in this journey of life together. So, let us make a conscious effort to spread joy and kindness every day, and watch as our lives become filled with an abundance of happiness and fulfillment.

Chapter 11: Sustaining Personal Growth in the Long Run

Overcoming Plateaus and Stagnation

Subchapter: Overcoming Plateaus and Stagnation

Introduction:

In our pursuit of a happy life, it is inevitable to encounter periods of stagnation and plateaus. These moments can leave us feeling stuck, demotivated, and unsure of how to move forward. However, it's important to remember that plateaus are not permanent, and with the right strategies, we can overcome them and continue on our journey towards a joyful existence. In this subchapter, we will explore effective techniques to navigate through plateaus and reignite the spark within us.

1. Recognize the Plateau: The first step towards overcoming a plateau is to recognize and acknowledge its existence. Reflect on your current state and identify the signs of stagnation. Are you lacking enthusiasm, feeling unchallenged, or experiencing a lack of progress? Awareness allows you to take control and make necessary changes.

2. Set New Goals: Plateaus often occur when we become complacent with our achievements. To break free, set new goals that challenge and inspire you. Whether it's learning a new skill, pursuing a passion project, or setting personal growth targets, having a clear direction will reignite your motivation and provide a fresh sense of purpose.

3.   Embrace   Change:
Routines can be comforting, but they can also lead to stagnation. Embrace change and step outside your comfort zone. Seek new experiences, explore different perspectives, and welcome challenges. Change stimulates personal growth and opens doors to exciting opportunities.

4.   Seek   Inspiration:
During plateaus, finding inspiration becomes crucial. Surround yourself with positive influences, whether it's reading books, listening to motivational podcasts, or connecting with like-minded individuals. Seek out role models who have overcome similar plateaus and learn from their experiences.

5.   Cultivate   Self-Discipline:
Overcoming plateaus requires discipline and consistency. Create a routine that fosters personal growth and commit to it. Break tasks into smaller, manageable steps, and celebrate the progress you make along the way. Remember, even small actions can lead to significant breakthroughs.

6.   Embrace   Failure:
Failure is an integral part of growth. Instead of fearing it, embrace failure as a valuable learning opportunity. Understand that setbacks are temporary and can provide valuable lessons. Use them as stepping stones towards progress and adapt your approach accordingly.

Conclusion:
Plateaus are not roadblocks but rather invitations to elevate ourselves and explore new horizons. By recognizing plateaus, setting new goals, embracing change, seeking inspiration, cultivating self-discipline, and embracing failure, we can overcome stagnation and continue our

journey towards a happy and fulfilling life. Remember, plateaus are temporary, and with the right mindset and strategies, you can break free and liberate your life.

Developing a Supportive Network

In our journey towards a happy life, one of the most crucial aspects is developing a supportive network. Surrounding ourselves with positive and uplifting individuals can make a world of difference in our overall well-being and success. This subchapter will explore the importance of building a supportive network and provide practical strategies to cultivate strong relationships that contribute to a joyful existence.

Human beings are inherently social creatures, and we thrive when we have a network of people who genuinely care about our happiness and success. A supportive network acts as a safety net during challenging times, providing emotional support, guidance, and encouragement. Whether it's family, friends, or mentors, having a support system can help us navigate through life's obstacles with more ease and resilience.

To develop a supportive network, we must first identify the kind of relationships we desire. Reflect on the qualities you seek in your support system – individuals who inspire, motivate, and uplift you. Surrounding yourself with like-minded people who share similar goals and values can create a positive environment that fosters personal growth.

Building a supportive network requires proactive effort. Start by reaching out to people who align with your aspirations and interests. Attend social gatherings, networking events, or join communities and organizations that resonate with your passions. Engage in meaningful conversations, listen attentively, and show genuine interest in others. Building rapport and trust takes time, so be patient and persistent.

Additionally, developing a supportive network involves reciprocation. Be willing to offer support and encouragement to others in your network. Celebrate their successes, lend a helping hand when needed, and provide a listening ear. By nurturing these relationships, you create a mutually beneficial environment where everyone thrives.

Remember that a supportive network is not limited to physical interactions. In today's digital age, we have access to online communities and social media platforms that can serve as valuable resources for building connections. Engaging in online discussions, participating in webinars, and joining virtual groups centered around personal development can expand your network and provide a sense of belonging.

Ultimately, developing a supportive network is an ongoing process. It requires consistent effort, nurturing, and the willingness to invest time and energy in building meaningful connections. By surrounding yourself with individuals who genuinely care about your happiness and success, you create a strong foundation for a joyful existence. So, take the necessary steps to cultivate and expand your support system, and watch as your life transforms into one filled with love, support, and happiness.

Embracing Change and Adaptability

In our journey towards a joyful existence, one of the most crucial skills we can cultivate is the ability to embrace change and adaptability. Change is an inevitable part of life, and those who can navigate it with grace and resilience often find themselves leading happier and more fulfilling lives.

Change can come in various forms – from minor shifts in our daily routines to major life transitions. It is our response to these changes that determines whether they become opportunities for growth or sources of stress. By developing a mindset of openness and flexibility, we can learn to embrace change as a natural and necessary part of our personal development.

Adaptability is the key to thriving in an ever-changing world. When we resist change, we create unnecessary suffering for ourselves. Instead of resisting, we can choose to see change as an invitation to explore new possibilities and expand our horizons. By embracing change, we open ourselves up to new experiences, opportunities, and perspectives that can enrich our lives in unexpected ways.

One powerful strategy for embracing change is cultivating a growth mindset. This mindset recognizes that our abilities and intelligence can be developed through dedication and hard work. Rather than viewing challenges as obstacles, we see them as opportunities to learn and grow. Adopting a growth mindset allows us to approach change with curiosity and optimism, enabling us to adapt and thrive in any situation.

Another essential aspect of embracing change is practicing self-compassion. Change can often trigger feelings of uncertainty, fear, and self-doubt. By treating ourselves with kindness and understanding during times of transition, we can build resilience and inner strength. Embracing change requires self-acceptance and a willingness to let go of old patterns and beliefs that no longer serve us.

In this subchapter, we will explore various strategies and exercises that can help us cultivate adaptability and embrace change. We will delve into the importance of self-reflection, mindfulness, and gratitude in navigating life's transitions. By incorporating these practices into our daily lives, we can develop the resilience and flexibility needed to lead a happy and fulfilling existence.

Remember, change is not something to be feared or avoided; it is an opportunity for growth and self-discovery. By embracing change and cultivating adaptability, we can liberate ourselves from the shackles of resistance and create a life filled with joy, purpose, and fulfillment.

Continuing the Journey of Personal Development

In the pursuit of a happy life, personal development is an ongoing journey that requires dedication, self-reflection, and a commitment to growth. It is a process that empowers individuals to unlock their full potential and live a joyful existence. As we embark on this journey, it is important to recognize that personal development is not a destination but a continuous evolution.

One of the key aspects of continuing the journey of personal development is self-awareness. Understanding ourselves on a deeper level allows us to identify our strengths, weaknesses, and areas for improvement. By gaining this insight, we can set realistic goals and develop strategies to overcome obstacles that may hinder our happiness. It also helps us to align our actions and values, ensuring that we are living an authentic and meaningful life.

Another vital component is the willingness to step out of our comfort zones. Growth and transformation occur when we challenge ourselves and embrace new experiences. It is through these unfamiliar territories that we discover our true potential, learn valuable life lessons, and develop resilience. Stepping out of our comfort zones also opens doors to opportunities we may have never imagined, leading us to a more fulfilling and happy life.

Continuing the journey of personal development also involves cultivating a growth mindset. This mindset allows us to view failures and setbacks as learning opportunities rather than roadblocks. By reframing our perspective, we can bounce back stronger, adapt to change, and embrace challenges with optimism. A growth mindset fuels our motivation and drives us towards continuous improvement and personal growth, ultimately contributing to our overall happiness.

Additionally, seeking support and surrounding ourselves with like-minded individuals is crucial in this journey. Connecting with a community of individuals who share similar goals and values provides a support system, accountability, and encouragement. It allows us to learn from others' experiences, gain valuable insights, and foster meaningful relationships. Together, we can inspire and uplift one another, creating an environment that nurtures personal growth and happiness.

In conclusion, continuing the journey of personal development is essential for a happy life. It requires self-awareness, stepping out of our comfort zones, cultivating a growth mindset, and seeking support. Embracing personal development as an ongoing journey empowers individuals to live a more joyful and fulfilling existence. As we continue on this path, let us remember that personal growth is not a destination, but a lifelong adventure.

Chapter 12: Conclusion

Recap of Key Strategies for Personal Development

In our journey towards a joyful existence, personal development plays a crucial role. It empowers us to liberate our lives from the shackles of negativity, self-doubt, and unfulfillment. This subchapter serves as a recap, summarizing the key strategies for personal development that we have explored throughout this book, "Liberate Your Life: Personal Development Strategies for a Joyful Existence."

1. Self-awareness: The foundation of personal development lies in understanding oneself. Take time to reflect on your values, strengths, and weaknesses. By embracing self-awareness, you can make conscious choices aligned with your true desires and aspirations.

2. Goal setting: Setting clear and achievable goals provides direction and purpose to your personal development journey. Break your larger goals into smaller, manageable steps, and celebrate each milestone along the way.

3. Positive mindset: Cultivate a positive mindset by focusing on gratitude, affirmations, and self-compassion. Challenge negative self-talk and replace it with empowering thoughts. Embrace failures as opportunities for growth and learn to see setbacks as temporary obstacles rather than permanent roadblocks.

4. Continuous learning: Commit to a lifelong journey of learning and personal growth. Seek new knowledge, acquire new skills, and explore different perspectives. Embrace change and adapt to new situations, allowing yourself to evolve and thrive.

5. Healthy habits: Take care of your physical, mental, and emotional well-being. Prioritize self-care activities such as exercise, healthy eating, meditation, and quality sleep. Surround yourself with a supportive network of friends and family who uplift and inspire you.

6. Time management: Efficiently managing your time is essential for personal development. Prioritize your tasks, eliminate distractions, and create a schedule that allows for both productivity and leisure. Remember to take breaks and recharge to maintain a healthy work-life balance.

7. Embracing challenges: Instead of avoiding challenges, embrace them as opportunities for growth. Step out of your comfort zone, confront your fears, and embrace new experiences. Each challenge you overcome will strengthen your resilience and expand your capabilities.

8. Cultivating gratitude: Gratitude is a powerful tool for personal development. Regularly express gratitude for the blessings in your life, both big and small. This practice shifts your focus towards the positive aspects of your existence, fostering a happier and more fulfilled life.

Remember, personal development is a lifelong journey. Embrace these key strategies and integrate them into your daily life to experience a joyful existence. By investing in your personal growth, you can liberate yourself from limitations and unlock your true potential. Start today and embark on a transformative journey towards a happier life.

Final Thoughts on Liberating Your Life

In the journey of life, happiness is the ultimate goal for everyone. We all yearn for a joyful existence, where we can live freely and unburdened by the obstacles that hold us back. Throughout this book, "Liberate Your Life: Personal Development Strategies for a Joyful Existence," we have explored various strategies and principles to help you achieve this state of liberation. Now, as we come to the end of this enlightening journey, let us reflect on some final thoughts that can truly transform your life.

First and foremost, remember that happiness is a choice. It is not something that can be obtained from external sources or material possessions. True happiness comes from within, from embracing gratitude, cultivating positive thoughts, and nurturing meaningful relationships. It is about finding contentment in the present moment.

To liberate your life, it is essential to let go of the past. We often carry the weight of past regrets, grudges, or failures, preventing us from moving forward. Embrace forgiveness, both towards others and yourself. Release the burden of the past, and you will find yourself empowered to create a brighter future.

Another crucial aspect of liberating your life is to embrace self-discovery. Take the time to understand yourself, your passions, and your purpose. Explore your strengths and weaknesses, and invest in personal growth. When you align your actions with your authentic self, you will experience a profound sense of fulfillment.

Remember, liberating your life does not mean living a life devoid of challenges. It means developing resilience and embracing change. Life is a series of ups and downs, but it is how we navigate through them that defines our happiness. Embrace setbacks as opportunities for growth and learning, and you will find yourself better equipped to face any adversity that comes your way.

Lastly, liberating your life requires patience and perseverance. Rome wasn't built in a day, and neither will your journey towards a joyful existence. Stay committed to your personal development, and embrace the process. Celebrate small victories along the way, and never lose sight of the ultimate goal – a truly happy life.

As we conclude this chapter and this book, we want to remind you that the power to liberate your life lies within you. Embrace the principles and strategies shared throughout this book, and let them guide you towards a life filled with joy, purpose, and contentment. Remember, you have the ability to create the life you desire – a life of liberation and happiness.

Embracing a Joyful Existence Moving Forward

In our relentless pursuit of happiness, we often forget that joy is not a destination but a state of being. It is not something we can find in external circumstances but rather a choice we make each day. Embracing a joyful existence is not about waiting for the perfect moment or achieving certain goals; it is about finding contentment and gratitude in the present moment.

Moving forward in life with a focus on joy requires a shift in perspective. Instead of constantly chasing after happiness, we must learn to appreciate the little moments of joy that come our way. It is about finding joy in simple things like a warm cup of coffee in the morning, a smile from a loved one, or a beautiful sunset. By recognizing and cherishing these moments, we can cultivate a deep sense of happiness that is not dependent on external circumstances.

One of the key strategies for embracing a joyful existence is practicing gratitude. Gratitude allows us to see the beauty and abundance that already exists in our lives. By focusing on what we have rather than what we lack, we can experience a profound sense of joy and contentment. Keeping a gratitude journal or simply taking a few moments each day to reflect on the things we are grateful for can have a transformative effect on our happiness levels.

Another important aspect of embracing a joyful existence is letting go of negativity and embracing positivity. Negative thoughts and emotions can weigh us down and prevent us from experiencing true joy. By cultivating a positive mindset and surrounding ourselves with positive influences, we can create a life filled with happiness and fulfillment.

Lastly, embracing a joyful existence requires us to prioritize self-care and self-love. Taking care of our physical, mental, and emotional well-being is essential for experiencing true joy in life. This can be achieved through activities such as exercise, meditation, spending time in nature, pursuing hobbies, and nurturing meaningful relationships.

In conclusion, embracing a joyful existence moving forward is about choosing to find joy in the present moment, practicing gratitude, embracing positivity, and prioritizing self-care. By adopting these strategies and making joy a priority in our lives, we can create a happy and fulfilling existence for ourselves. Remember, joy is not a destination; it is a journey that we can embark on every day. So, let us choose joy and embrace the beauty of life.

Milton Keynes UK
Ingram Content Group UK Ltd.
UKHW020930231123
433129UK00016B/863